Healthy Five Ingredient Recipes

Hannie P. Scott

ISBN-13: 978-1546720461
ISBN-10: 1546720464

My Free Gift to You!

55
Quick
&
Easy
Recipes

hannie p. scott

To download your free gift, simply visit:

www.hanniepscott.com/freegift

TABLE OF CONTENTS

Abbreviations

oz = ounce

fl oz = fluid ounce

tsp = teaspoon

tbsp = tablespoon

ml = milliliter

c = cup

pt = pint

qt = quart

gal = gallon

L = liter

Conversions

1/2 fl oz = 3 tsp = 1 tbsp = 15 ml

1 fl oz = 2 tbsp = 1/8 c = 30 ml

2 fl oz = 4 tbsp = 1/4 c = 60 ml

4 fl oz = 8 tbsp = 1/2 c = 118 ml

8 fl oz = 16 tbsp = 1 c = 236 ml

16 fl oz = 1 pt = 1/2 qt = 2 c = 473 ml

128 fl oz = 8 pt = 4 qt = 1 gal = 3.78 L

Introduction

Two years ago, I asked my readers what kind of recipe book they would like to see from me next. The overwhelming majority suggested I create a book filled with recipes with "just a few ingredients" and I loved the idea.

I, like many others, can feel overwhelmed when I see a page full of ingredients when I'm venturing into a new recipe. I created the *Five Ingredient Cookbook* and it has been my favorite and best-selling book yet. I love all the recipes in it, but I wanted to create a similar book that was healthier.

My health, the health of my family, and the health of my friends and readers is extremely important to me. This book is filled with recipes with simple, healthy ingredients that I hope you and your family will love as much as my family and I do!

Lemon Pepper Chicken

Servings: 4

What you need:

· 4 chicken breasts
· 1 cup of olive oil
· 2/3 cup lemon juice
· 2 cloves of garlic, minced
· 1 medium yellow onion, diced

What to do:

1. In a small bowl, whisk together the olive oil, lemon juice, and garlic. Stir in the onions.
2. Put the chicken into a large bowl and pour the lemon/oil mixture over it. Cover and refrigerate for several hours.
3. Place the chicken on a skillet or grill heated over medium heat and cook for 20 minutes, flipping halfway through cooking time, or until the center of the chicken is fully cooked.

Kale Chips

Servings: 4

What you need:

- 1 bunch of kale, washed and thoroughly dried
- 3 tbsp olive oil
- 2 tsp sea salt
- Juice from 1 lemon

What to do:

1. Preheat your oven to 350 degrees F.
2. Strip the kale from the stems and break it into pieces.
3. In a large bowl, combine the kale with the olive oil, salt, and lemon juice. Stir until the kale has somewhat wilted.
4. Spread the kale evenly onto a large baking sheet and bake for 20 minutes or until crispy.

Roasted Cauliflower

Servings: 4

What you need:

- 1 large head of cauliflower
- 3 tbsp olive oil
- 1 clove garlic, minced
- 1 tsp sea salt
- 1 tsp red pepper flakes

What to do:

1. Preheat your oven to 350 degrees F.
2. Trim the stem of the cauliflower so that it is even with the florets and can sit flat on a baking sheet.
3. In a small bowl, stir together the olive oil, garlic, salt, and red pepper flakes.
4. Lay the cauliflower on a baking sheet and brush the olive oil mixture all over the cauliflower.
5. Bake for 55 minutes or until tender.
6. Slice into wedges then serve.

Tex-Mex Eggs

Servings: 2

What you need:

- 4 eggs
- 1 cup black beans
- 1/2 cup salsa (no sugar)
- 1/2 avocado, cut into cubes
- 2 handfuls spinach

What to do:

1. Scramble the eggs in a skillet over medium heat.
2. When the eggs are set, stir in the black beans, salsa, and spinach. Cook until heated and spinach is wilted.
3. Before serving, top with avocado.

Overnight Oats

Servings: 1

What you need:

- 1/2 cup old fashioned oats
- 3/4 cup unsweetened almond milk
- 1 tsp pure maple syrup
- 1 tsp pure vanilla extract
- Fruit of your choice

What to do:

1. Add all of the ingredients to a glass jar, secure the lid, and shake well.
2. Refrigerate for at least 6 hours.
3. Shake well before eating.

Roasted Chick Peas

About 4 servings per can

What you need:

- 1 15-oz can of chick peas/garbanzo beans*
- 2 tbsp olive oil
- Seasonings of choice – ideas at the bottom of the page

What to do:

1. Drain and rinse the chick peas. Remove any loose skins.
2. Spread the peas out on a paper towel or clean dish towel and let them dry.
3. Preheat your oven to 400 degrees F and line a baking sheet with foil.
4. Place the peas in a large bowl and drizzle and toss them in olive oil and seasonings.
5. Pour them onto the baking sheet and spread them out evenly.
6. Bake for 30 minutes or until crunchy.

Seasoning Ideas:

- Sesame: 1 tsp sesame oil, 1 tsp garlic powder, 1 tsp sea salt, 1 tbsp sesame seeds
- Garlic: 2 tsp garlic powder, 1/2 tsp black pepper, 1/2 tsp salt
- Spicy Taco: 1 tsp ground cumin, 1 tsp chili powder, 1/2 tsp cayenne pepper, 1/2 tsp salt
- Ranch: 1 tbsp ranch seasoning

- Smokey: 1/2 tsp ancho chile powder, 1/2 tsp smoked paprika, 1/2 tsp garlic powder, 1/2 tsp cumin, 1/2 tsp pepper, 1/2 tsp salt, a pinch of cayenne

*I know you already know this but I'm saying it anyway, chick peas and garbanzo beans are the same thing.

Kale Salad

Servings: 6

What you need:

· 1 bunch of kale
· 1/4 cup lemon juice
· Salt, to taste
· 2 tbsp olive oil
· 1/2 yellow onion, thinly sliced

What to do:

1. Remove the stems from the kale and discard.
2. Tear the kale leaves into smaller pieces and wash and dry them thoroughly.
3. Place the kale in a large mixing bowl and drizzle it with lemon juice, salt, and olive oil.
4. Stir the kale with your hands, making sure to "massage" it really well. Do this for 5 minutes. The kale will wilt and turn a very dark green.
5. Toss in the thinly sliced onions and serve.

Cabbage Steaks

Servings: 4

What you need:

- 1 head of green cabbage, cut into 1" thick slices
- 2 tbsp olive oil
- 3 cloves of garlic, minced
- Salt and pepper, to taste

What to do:

1. Preheat your oven to 400 degrees F and spray a baking sheet with nonstick cooking spray.
2. Brush each side of the cabbage slices with olive oil and lay them out on the baking sheet.
3. Place a small amount of minced garlic on each cabbage slice and sprinkle with salt and pepper.
4. Roast for 30 minutes then carefully flip the cabbage steaks and cook for another 20 minutes.

Prosciutto Wrapped Asparagus

Makes 12 Spears

What you need:

· 12 asparagus spears
· 6 slices of prosciutto
· Butter or nonstick spray

What to do:

1. Snap off the ends of the asparagus spears.
2. Cut the prosciutto into two halves.
3. Wrap each asparagus spear in prosciutto.
4. Heat about a half a tbsp of butter in a large nonstick skillet.
5. In batches, cook the spears for 1-2 minutes on each side. Serve immediately.

Buffalo Chicken Pieces

Servings: 2-4

What you need:

·   3-4 chicken breasts, chopped into small pieces
·   Salt and pepper
·   2 tbsp olive oil
·   Frank's Buffalo Sauce

What to do:

1.   Season the chicken pieces with salt and pepper and sauté them in 2 tbsp of olive oil heated over medium heat.
2.   Cook the chicken, turning and stirring every couple of minutes, until it is cooked through and slightly crisp on the outside.
3.   Remove the chicken from the pan and drizzle with Frank's Buffalo Sauce.

Taco Salad

Servings: 4

What you need:

– mushroom substitute

- 1 lb ground beef
- 2 tbsp taco seasoning
- 15 oz can of red kidney beans, drained and rinsed – use no salt added if preferred
- 1 cup chopped lettuce
- A handful of cherry tomatoes, halved

What to do:

1. Brown the ground beef and drain off the fat.
2. Over medium low heat, stir in the taco seasoning and add a little water if needed.
3. Stir in the drained kidney beans and cook for 3-5 minutes until the beans are heated completely.
4. Serve over chopped lettuce and top with cherry tomatoes.

Taco Seasoning

Makes 1 cup of seasoning, enough for 8 lbs of ground meat

What you need:

- 2/3 cup chili powder
- 3 tbsp cumin
- 1 tbsp salt
- 2 tsp garlic powder
- 2 tsp onion powder

What to do:

1. Mix all of the ingredients together and store in an airtight jar or container.
2. Use 2 tbsp per 1 lb of ground meat.

Stuffed Peppers

Servings: 8

What you need:

- 4 bell peppers
- 1 lb ground beef
- 2 tbsp taco seasoning
- 1 can of black beans, drained and rinsed
- 1 can of rotel tomatoes

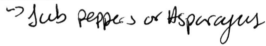

sub mushrooms

→ *Sub peppers or Asparagus*

What to do:

1. Preheat your oven to 375 degrees F.
2. Cut the tops off of the bell peppers and scoop out the seeds.
3. Cook the ground beef until brown then drain off the fat. Stir in the taco seasoning and a small amount of water, about a 1/2 of a cup.
4. Stir the rotel tomatoes and drained black beans into the taco meat.
5. Scoop the taco mixture into each pepper.
6. Bake for 30 minutes then serve.

Deviled Eggs

Servings: 8

What you need:

· 8 hard-boiled eggs
· 3 tbsp hummus
· Salt and pepper, to taste
· Paprika, for garnishing

What to do:

1. Peel the eggs and slice each of them in half lengthwise.
2. Gently remove the yolks and place them into a bowl.
3. Add the hummus, salt, and pepper. Stir everything together until combined.
4. Scoop spoonfuls of the yolk mixture back on to the egg whites.
5. Sprinkle with paprika.

Spinach Parmesan Pasta

Servings: 4

What you need:

- 8 oz whole wheat vermicelli
- 3 tbsp olive oil
- 2 cloves of garlic, minced
- 6 cups baby spinach
- 1 cup freshly grated parmesan cheese

What to do:

1. Add the pasta to a large pot of boiling salted water and cook until al dente, according to package directions. Drain the pasta, reserving 1/2 cup of the pasta water. Set aside the pasta and the reserved water.
2. Using the same pot, heat the olive oil over medium heat. Add the garlic and cook for 3 minutes.
3. Add in the pasta and the spinach and gently toss and cook until the spinach is wilted. If the pasta begins to dry out add a small amount of the reserved pasta water.
4. Stir in the cheese and serve.

Spinach Macaroni and Cheese

Servings: 4

What you need:

· 8 oz whole wheat elbow macaroni
· 2 cups shredded sharp cheddar cheese
· 1/2 cup plain, full fat Greek yogurt
· 2 cups fresh spinach
· Salt and pepper, to taste

What to do:

1. Cook the macaroni according to the package directions to al dente.
2. Place the spinach leaves in a strainer and pour the pasta over the spinach to drain. This will wilt the spinach. Reserve 1/2 cup of pasta water.
3. Return the cooked pasta and wilted spinach to the pot.
4. Add 1/4 cup of the reserved pasta water to the pot and stir in the cheese until it is melted. Stir in the Greek yogurt, salt, and pepper until smooth and creamy.
5. If needed, stir in more pasta water to get it to the right consistency.

Pesto Chicken Stuffed Peppers

Servings: 6

What you need:

· 6 red, orange, and/or yellow bell peppers
· 2 chicken breasts, cooked and shredded
· 10-oz mozzarella cheese, shredded
· 1 cup cooked quinoa
· 1 6-oz (approx.) jar of pesto

What to do:

1. Turn your broiler on high and place the bell peppers under the broiler for 5 minutes on each side until the skin begins to blister and turn black. Remove from oven and set aside.
2. Preheat the oven to 350 degrees F.
3. In a mixing bowl, combine the shredded chicken, 1 cup of shredded cheese, quinoa, and pesto. Stir to combine.
4. Slice the peppers in half length-wise and remove the membranes and seeds. Add a heaping 1/4 cup of the chicken mixture to each pepper and top with additional cheese.
5. Bake for 10 minutes then serve.

Spicy Mustard Chicken Thighs

Servings: 2

What you need:

- 3 tbsp spicy brown mustard
- 2 tsp chopped fresh thyme
- 1/2 tsp salt
- 2 lbs boneless skinless chicken thighs

What to do:

1. Preheat your oven to 375 degrees F and spray a large rimmed baking sheet with cooking spray.
2. Whisk together the mustard, thyme, and salt in a large bowl.
3. Add the chicken thighs to the bowl and toss to coat them well.
4. Arrange the chicken on the baking sheet.
5. Roast the chicken until it is cooked through, about 45 minutes.

Tomato Basil Bisque

Servings: 4

What you need:

- 10 roma tomatoes, halved
- 2 yellow onions, quartered
- 4 cloves of garlic
- 3 tbsp olive oil
- 1/3 cup roughly chopped fresh basil

What to do:

1. Place the tomatoes, onions, and garlic into a large bowl and drizzle with the olive oil and season with salt and pepper, if desired. Stir to coat.
2. Pour the vegetables onto a large baking tray and roast at 450 degrees F for 30 minutes. Stir halfway through cooking time.
3. Let cool for 5-10 minutes.
4. Place the roasted vegetables and the basil in a blender and blend until smooth.
5. Heat soup on the stove, if necessary.

Chicken Feta Pasta

Servings: 4

What you need:

· 2 tbsp extra virgin olive oil
· 2 lbs boneless, skinless chicken breasts, cut in half
· 2 14-oz cans of Italian diced tomatoes
· 1 lb whole wheat fettucine pasta
· 4 oz crumbled

What to do:

1. In a large saucepan over medium high, heat the olive oil then add in the chicken. Season with salt and pepper if desired. Cook the chicken for 8 minutes on one side, flip over and cook the other side for 5 minutes.
2. Add in the diced tomatoes and 2 cups of water. Stir in the uncooked pasta and cook without the lid for 5 minutes. Cover and cook for another 10 minutes.
3. Remove the lid and add the feta and stir.
4. Serve warm.

Grilled Orange Balsamic Brussels Sprouts

Servings: 4

What you need:

- · 1 lb fresh Brussels sprouts, washed
- · 1/4 cup olive oil
- · 3 tbsp fresh squeezed orange juice
- · 1 1/2 tsp balsamic vinegar
- · 1 tbsp fresh chopped oregano

What to do:

1. Combine all of the ingredients in a large bowl with a lid and stir.
2. Marinate for at least 2 hours in the refrigerator.
3. Preheat your grill to high. Horizontally place the Brussels sprouts on skewers (side to side, not stem to top). I put 4-5 Brussels sprouts on each skewer.
4. Place the skewers on the grill and cook for 4 minutes then flip and cook for another 4 minutes.
5. Remove from grill and serve.

Zucchini Fritters

Servings: 6

What you need:

- 4 cups shredded zucchini
- 1/3 cup sliced green onions
- 2/3 cup almond flour
- 2 tbsp olive oil
- 2 large eggs

What to do:

1. Place the shredded zucchini in a colander over a bowl and sprinkle with salt. Let stand for 10 minutes then squeeze out as much liquid as possible with your hands. Place the squeezed out zucchini in a large bowl.
2. Add the flour, onions, and eggs to the bowl and season with salt and pepper, if desired. Stir to combine the mixture.
3. Heat the olive oil to a large skillet over medium heat.
4. Scoop the zucchini mixture into 3-tbsp mounds and place them into the hot skillet about 2 inches apart. Gently flatten them out. Work in batches. Cook for 2-3 minutes per side.
5. Transfer to paper towel lined plates then serve.

Garlic Prime Rib Roast

Servings: 8

What you need:

- 2 tbsp minced garlic
- 2 tbsp olive oil
- 2-3 sprigs fresh thyme
- 5 lb boneless prime rib roast
- Salt and pepper, to taste

What to do:

1. Mix together all of the ingredients but the roast.
2. Marinate the roast in the mixture overnight. I put my roast in a large roasting pan and poured the mixture over it, covered it with the lid, and refrigerated it overnight.
3. Two hours before you get ready to cook the roast, remove it from the refrigerator and let it come to room temperature.
4. Preheat your oven to 450 degrees F and roast uncovered for 15 minutes. Reduce the heat to 300 degrees and roast for 2 hours or until a thermometer reads 130-135 degrees F. It will be medium rare. For rare, cook to an internal temperature of 120-125 degrees F. For well done, cook to an internal temperature of 145 degrees F.

Pineapple Salsa Chicken

Servings: 6

What you need:

- 2 lbs boneless, skinless chicken breasts
- 1 16-oz jar of tomato salsa
- 1 20-oz can of pineapple chunks in 100% juice, juice reserved
- 3 medium zucchinis, diced

What to do:

1. Place the chicken breasts in your slow cooker and pour the salsa over them. Cook on high for 4 hours or on low for 6 hours. Shred the chicken.
2. Add in the pineapples with 3/4 cup of the canned juice and the zucchini and cook for another 30 minutes.

Baked Fajita Chicken

Servings: 4

What you need:

- 4 boneless skinless chicken breasts
- 1 red bell pepper, cut into strips
- 1 small onion, sliced
- 1 cup salsa
- 1 cup shredded cheese

What to do:

1. Preheat your oven to 400 degrees F.
2. Grease a 9x13 inch baking dish.
3. Lay each chicken breast into the baking dish and top with salsa.
4. Top the salsa with onion and peppers.
5. Bake for 30-40 minutes or until the chicken is fully cooked.
6. Top with cheese and bake for another 5 minutes.

Slow Cooker Ham

Servings: 12

What you need:

- 5 lb bone in ham
- 1 cup apple cider vinegar
- 3 tbsp dry mustard

What to do:

1. Place the ham in your slow cooker.
2. Press the dry mustard onto the ham.
3. Pour the apple cider vinegar into the bottom of the crock pot.
4. Cook on low for 8 hours, flipping over 1/2 way through cooking time.

Lemon Chicken with Asparagus

Servings: 4

What you need:

· 1 lb boneless skinless chicken breasts
· 2 tbsp butter
· 1 tsp lemon pepper seasoning
· 2 cups chopped asparagus
· 2 lemons, sliced

What to do:

1. Pound out the chicken breasts until they are 3/4 inch thick or cut them in half horizontally if they are really thick. Season breasts with salt and pepper, if desired.
2. Heat the butter in a large skillet over medium high heat. Add in the chicken and cook on each side for 5 minutes. Sprinkle each side with lemon pepper as you are cooking. When the chicken is golden brown and cooked all the way through, transfer it to a plate.
3. In the same pan, cook the asparagus over medium heat until bright green and starting to become tender, about 5 minutes. Remove from pan and set aside.
4. Melt a little bit of butter in the pan and place the sliced lemons in the pan and cook for a few minutes on each side until they begin to caramelize. Remove and set aside.
5. Layer the ingredients back in the skillet – asparagus, then chicken, then lemons. Heat for 4-5 minutes over medium low heat then serve.

Grilled Sesame Chicken

Servings: 4

What you need:

- 2 tbsp tomato paste
- 2 tbsp sesame seeds
- 1 tbsp sesame oil
- 2 tbsp soy sauce
- 4 chicken thigh filets

What to do:

1. Preheat your oven to 375 degrees F and line a baking sheet with parchment paper and set aside.
2. In a small bowl, whisk together the tomato paste, sesame seeds, sesame oil, and soy sauce.
3. Coat the chicken thighs with the mixture and arrange them on the prepared baking sheet.
4. Bake for 30 minutes and then serve.

Baked Chicken Parmesan

Servings: 6

What you need:

- 4 chicken breasts
- 1 24-oz organic pasta sauce
- 10-oz fresh mozzarella, sliced
- 1 1/2 cups panko bread crumbs
- 1/3 cup parmesan cheese, grated

What to do:

1. Preheat your oven to 350 degrees F and spray a baking dish with nonstick spray.
2. Place the chicken breasts in the dish and top with pasta sauce. Top the sauce with a layer of sliced mozzarella.
3. In a small bowl, stir together the panko and parmesan cheese. Sprinkle the mixture over the ingredients in the dish and cover with foil.
4. Bake for 40-50 minutes or until the chicken is cooked through.

BLT Lettuce Wraps

Servings: varies

What you need:

- Turkey Bacon
- Tomato slices
- Large lettuce leaves
- Mayonnaise, optional

What to do:

1. Cook the turkey bacon until crisp.
2. Lay out a lettuce leaf flat and place 2 strips of turkey bacon, a few slices of tomato, and mayonnaise (if using).
3. Roll up the lettuce into a wrap and enjoy!

Couscous and Eggs

Servings: 4-6

What you need:

- 2 cups couscous
- 2 cups water
- 2 tbsp olive oil
- 1 clove garlic, minced
- 1/2 cup parmesan cheese
- 4 to 6 eggs

What to do:

1. Spray a muffin pan with non-stick spray and break one egg into each cup (you won't fill up the whole pan). Bake at 375 degrees F for 15-18 minutes.
2. Place the water, olive oil, and garlic in a saucepan and bring to a boil. Once boiling, stir in the couscous and parmesan cheese, remove from heat, cover and let sit for 5 minutes.
3. Serve the eggs over the couscous.

Zucchini Spaghetti

Servings: 4

What you need:

- 1 lb lean ground beef
- 1 jar of organic, low sugar spaghetti sauce
- 4 small-medium zucchini

What to do:

1. Brown the ground beef in a large saucepan then drain off the fat. Pour in the spaghetti sauce, cover, and simmer on medium low heat for 20 minutes.
2. While the sauce is simmering, spiralizer the zucchini. If you don't have a spiralizer you could use a vegetable peeler to cut it into strips.
3. Place the zucchini noodles into the pan with the sauce and toss to coat. Heat for 2-3 minutes then serve.

Peanut Butter Energy Bites

Makes 12 bites

What you need:

· 2/3 cup creamy peanut butter
· 1/2 cup dark chocolate chips
· 1 cup old fashioned oats
· 1/2 cup ground flaxseeds
· 2 tbsp honey

What to do:

1. Combine the ingredients in a mixing bowl and stir together.
2. Cover and refrigerate for 30 minutes to harden a bit.
3. Roll into 12 bites. Store in an airtight container in the fridge if you aren't immediately eating them.

Sweet Potato Eggs

Servings: 4

What you need:

· 2 tsp coconut oil
· 1 sweet potato
· 4 eggs
· Shredded sharp cheddar cheese, optional
· Salt and pepper, to taste

What to do:

1. Grate or julienne the sweet potato.
2. Heat the coconut oil in a large cast iron skillet.
3. Once hot, cook the sweet potato in the pan until soft, 10-12 minutes. Spread the sweet potato evenly around the pan and create 4 wells for the eggs.
4. Turn your oven's broiler on high.
5. Crack the eggs into the wells and place the whole skillet in your oven and cook for 5 minutes. Sprinkle on the cheese, if using, then place back in the oven. Cook until the whites are set and the yolks are cooked to your liking.
6. Season with salt and pepper, then serve.

Black Bean Stew

Servings: 4

What you need:

- 3 15-oz cans of black beans with liquid
- 3 cups salsa
- 1/2 cup chopped fresh cilantro, plus extra for garnish
- 2 tsp ground cumin
- 1 clove garlic, minced

What to do:

1. Stir the ingredients together in a medium saucepan and heat over medium heat until simmering. Reduce heat to low and cover and cook for 20 minutes.
2. Serve topped with extra cilantro as garnish.

Tomato and Artichoke Chicken

Servings: 2

What you need:

- 1 lb chicken thighs
- 8-oz jar of artichoke hearts
- 1 cup cherry tomatoes
- 2 tbsp butter

What to do:

1. Preheat your oven to 375 degrees F.
2. Add all of the ingredients to a baking dish and bake for 30 minutes or until the chicken is cooked through.
3. Remove from oven and let sit for 10 minutes then serve.

Baked Eggs with Kale and Sweet Potato

Servings: 2

What you need:

- 2 medium sweet potatoes
- 1 tbsp olive oil
- 1 cup chopped kale
- 2 eggs

What to do:

1. Bake the sweet potatoes for 1 hour (or until soft) at 400 degrees F. Once the potatoes have cooled enough to handle, scoop out the insides to a bowl and mash them.
2. In a cast iron skillet over medium heat, add the olive oil and mashed sweet potatoes. Stir and somewhat press the sweet potato down.
3. Add in 1 cup of chopped kale and cook until soft.
4. Crack 2 eggs into the skillet and place in a 400 degree oven and bake for 12-15 minutes until the egg whites are set but the yolks are still runny.

Lemon Garlic Chicken

Servings: 4

What you need:

- 4 lemons
- 3 heads of garlic
- 1 whole chicken, about 5 lbs
- Fresh rosemary
- Cajun seasoning

What to do:

1. Cut the lemons and heads of garlic in half and lay them in the bottom of your slow cooker.
2. Add in 2-3 sprigs of fresh rosemary.
3. Removed the insides of the chicken and rinse then pat dry.
4. Season the chicken inside and out with Cajun seasoning.
5. Place the chicken on top of the lemons and garlic in your slow cooker.
6. Cook on high for 4 hours or until the chicken reaches 165 degrees F. Baste the chicken every hour.

Baked Salmon

Servings: 12

What you need:

- 6 6-oz sockeye salmon fillets
- Salt, to taste
- 1/2 cup Thai chili sauce, plus 2 tbsp
- 3 tbsp chopped green onions
- Cooking spray

What to do:

1. Place the salmon fillets in a large baking dish in an even layer.
2. Sprinkle the fillets with salt and top each fillet with 1 tbsp of chili sauce. Cover and marinate in the refrigerator for 2 hours or up to 24 hours.
3. Position your oven rack about 6 inches below the heat source and turn on your broiler.
4. Line a large baking sheet with foil, spray the foil with cooking spray, and place the salmon skin side down (if skin was left on). Coat with the remaining marinade from the dish.
5. Broil for 8 minutes. Remove and brush the fillets with the remaining 2 tbsp of chili sauce. Broil for another 5 minutes or until caramelized.
6. Serve hot, garnished with green onions.

Quinoa Pizza Crust

Makes a 9-inch pizza crust

What you need:

· 3/4 cup quinoa
· 1/4 cup of water, plus extra for soaking
· 1/2 tsp baking powder
· 1/2 tsp salt
· 2 tbsp olive oil

What to do:

1. Place the quinoa in a bowl and cover it with water. Use enough water to where it's covering the quinoa by about an inch. Soak overnight or 6-8 hours.
2. When you're ready to make the crust, preheat your oven to 425 degrees F and line a 9-inch cake pan with parchment paper.
3. Drizzle 1 tbsp of olive oil onto the parchment paper and spread it around to coat the paper well.
4. Rinse the quinoa then add it to a blender or food processor. Add 1/4 cup water, baking powder, salt, and 1 tbsp olive oil. Blend on high until smooth.
5. Pour batter into the prepared pan. Top with desired toppings and bake for 13-15 minutes.
6. Remove from the oven and let it cool for a couple minutes then slice and serve.

Vegetarian Mexican Quinoa Stuffed Peppers

Servings: 6

What you need:

- 6 medium bell peppers, tops cut off and seeds and insides removed
- 2 cans of black beans, rinsed and drained
- 3 cups cooked quinoa
- 8 oz shredded pepper jack cheese
- 1 cup salsa

What to do:

1. Preheat your oven to 350 degrees F and arrange the peppers in a large baking dish, open side facing up.
2. In a large mixing bowl, stir together the black beans, quinoa, 1 1/2 cups of shredded cheese, and salsa.
3. Evenly spoon the mixture into the peppers. Sprinkle the tops with the remaining cheese.
4. Bake for 30 minutes then serve.

White Chicken Chili

Servings: 4-6

What you need:

· 6 cups chicken broth
· 4 cups cooked and shredded chicken
· 2 15-oz cans of great northern beans, drained and rinsed
· 2 cups salsa verde
· 1 tbsp ground cumin

What to do:

1. Place all of the ingredients in a medium saucepan over medium high heat. Bring to a boil then cover and reduce heat and simmer for 20 minutes. You could also do this in a crock pot and use raw chicken, just cook for 4-6 hours on low, then shred the chicken before serving.

Low Carb Broccoli Cheese Soup

Servings: 4

What you need:

- 4 cups of broccoli florets
- 2 cloves of garlic, minced
- 3 1/2 cups chicken broth
- 1 cup heavy cream
- 3 cups shredded cheddar cheese

What to do:

1. In a large pot over medium heat, sauté the garlic for one minute. Add in the broth, cream, and chopped broccoli. Bring ALMOST to a boil then reduce heat and simmer for 15 minutes or until broccoli is tender.
2. Add in the shredded cheese and stir until melted. Remove from heat and serve.

About the Author

Hannie P. Scott, Full-Time Mom and Food Blogger

Driven by her desire for cooking for others (and herself), Hannie spends a lot of time in the kitchen! She enjoys sharing her love of food with the world by creating "no-nonsense" recipe books that anyone can use to make delicious meals.

Hannie attended the University of Southern Mississippi and received a Bachelor's degree in Nutrition & Dietetics. She enjoys cooking and experimenting with food. She hopes to inspire readers and help them build confidence in their cooking. All Hannie's recipes are easy-to-prepare with easy-to-acquire ingredients.

For more recipes, cooking tips, and Hannie's blog, visit:

www.Hanniepscott.com

Notes

Notes

Notes

Notes

Notes

Notes